Water Cycle

Donna Marie Pitino

ABRAMS & COMPANY Publishers, Inc.
Waterbury, CT

Contents

Imagine you are an astronaut in outer space. You look down at the Earth. What do you see?

Lots and lots of water!

Water covers more than $\frac{2}{3}$ of the Earth.

Water can be found in oceans, rivers, and lakes. It is even frozen in icebergs!

Where else can water be found?

All living things need water. People and animals drink water. Farmers water their crops.

We use water to clean things. We even use water to make electricity!

How else can water be used?

People, plants, and animals use lots of water, but the amount of water on Earth stays about the same.

How can that be?

Try this experiment to find out!

Place a glass of water in a sunny spot. Measure the water level every day. What happens?

The water level goes down a little bit each day. Finally, the water disappears!

When water gets warmer, it changes from a *liquid* to a *gas*. The water becomes *water vapor* and rises into the air. This process is called *evaporation*.

Now fill a glass with ice and water. Wait a few minutes. Look at the outside of the glass. What do you see?

Water!

When air gets colder, the water vapor in the air turns back into liquid water. This process is called *condensation*.

Evaporation and condensation are nature's way of *recycling* water, or using it over and over again.

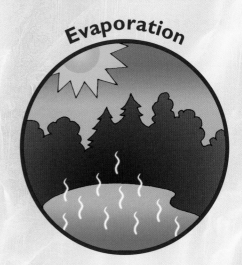

Evaporation

Heat from the Sun evaporates water in oceans, rivers, lakes, and ponds.

Collection

Precipitation refills the oceans, rivers, lakes, and ponds.

Condensation

As the water vapor rises, it cools and condenses into tiny drops of water. Those water drops form a cloud.

Precipitation

When the water drops get big enough, they fall back to Earth as rain or snow.

This natural recycling process is called the *water cycle*.

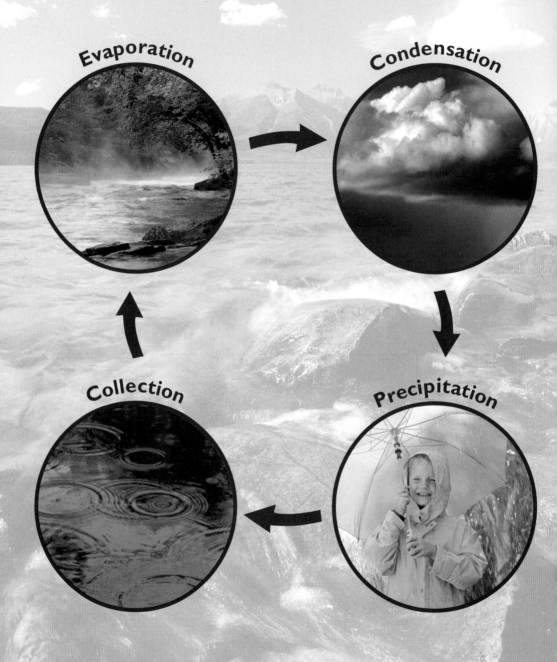

Evaporation

Condensation

Collection

Precipitation